Love After Life

How I defeated grief and kept my relationship with my soul-mate strong and joyful after she passed from the physical.

by William J. Murray

Irene,

You brought me to life the day we met.
I love you forever and for always.

Bill

You may notice that I still write about Irene in the present tense,
as if she is still with me; that is because I fully believe she is.
- William J. Murray

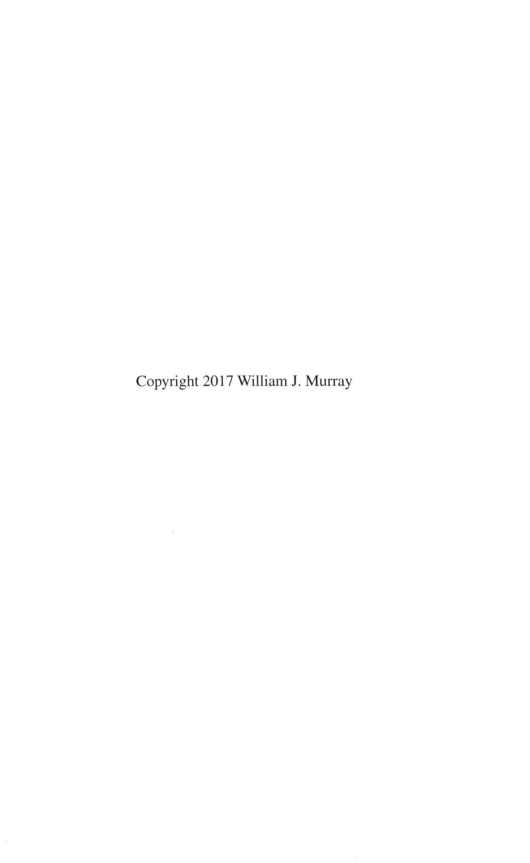

Table of Contents

Prologue

This is not a description of "moving on" from that relationship, but rather of moving forward in that relationship and meeting the formidable challenge of continuing even through her death, and even through the dark trials of profound grief. This book is for those that share an eternal commitment to their departed loved one and choose not to "move on," but rather choose to embrace a transdimensional relationship as best they can until fully reunited with their soul mate.

A few notes are in order before you purchase or read this book. First and foremost, if you don't believe an afterlife exists, the information in this book will likely be of no benefit. I'm not setting out to prove to anyone that anything I write in this book about the qualities of afterlife existence is true; there is already plenty of information and research out there the reader can access in order to make up his or her own mind. I will direct the reader to those books, sites and other media that proved helpful in validating certain things I believe, which can serve as the intellectual and evidential foundation for the process described in this book.

This book describes the grief-eliminating and transdimensional relationship-building process I found and developed through my personal experience and nothing more. The focus of this book is to provide the reader with an account of how I found my way back to feeling fulfilled, whole, happy and joyful in continuing my relationship with my soul-mate after she died. The entire premise of my attempt to accomplish this restoration rested upon my deep knowledge that there could be no one else for me and that the only way I could go on was by finding some way to "reconnect" in a fulfilling way while still being completely in love with and being fully committed to her. This decision may not be for everyone.

Chapter 1
Our Time Together On Earth

I'd like to spend just a little time talking about our life before she passed from this world. My purpose in this chapter is to let the reader know that what we have is no casual love. What I mean by "soul-mate" is that we are romantic, eternal soul-mates – we complete each other in a very profound sense and our connection is intense, deep, broad and passionate – and yes, I speak of her in the present tense because I fully believe she is still with me.

The night before we met in a small town in Texas in 1990, Irene had a dream that she wrote down in her journal. In the dream she had a new boyfriend named "Bill" and she and Bill were standing by an old black truck, even though she couldn't see his face. That day she got a letter in response to her personals ad in a local thrift paper from a "Bill" - me.

Before taking out that ad Irene had prayed to God to give her a true love instead of her having boyfriends that wouldn't commit themselves to her or her three young children. I answered the ad after that paper had been lying around a week or so only because she had pretty much described me as the kind of man she was looking for – even down to the physical description.

She called me up. We both liked how each other sounded, and we met halfway between the city I lived in and where she lived, which was about three small country towns away, at a public place. What made her immediately so interesting to me was her blunt, no-nonsense honesty. She had all she could take of games so she just laid out the her story and said that if any of it gave me pause, best just to get it over then and there.

She even brought her children with her so I would get the full scope of what was going to be involved in a relationship with her - and that was on our first meeting. I was totally amazed by her personality and her up-front directness.

We both had two marriages that had ended well before we met. We both had been mistreated by our spouses and had our share of misfortune – enough to give anyone pause and a big dose of mistrust. Personally I had decided not to ever marry again and she had all but given up on "true love."

Five days from when we met, we were so much in love that it was as if everything before had simply ceased to exist. We couldn't sleep when we were around each other. We thought of each other constantly when apart. Her children took right to me and I to them. Two weeks after we met we felt like we had always known each other and had always been together. It was, as they say, like coming home.

I'm not going to write here about all the crazy, magical, unbelievable things that happened to us over the course of our twenty-seven years together. That's not what this book is about. We went through our ups and downs, but as we met every challenge our feelings for each other did nothing but grow deeper and stronger. We each knew (and still know) what the other is thinking without a word or even a glance, reading each other's mind without trying. Our humor and views were and are perfectly suited for each other; we enjoy doing just about anything together. We share a deep belief in a particular view of God and the afterlife you'll hear more about later.

The thing about Irene and me is that we had our physical life and existence together figured out (at least as far as we were concerned); we had found how to be completely, totally satisfied. We are complete and whole together. Years before she passed we would tell each other that we had already won this life; and if we died, we could die completely and totally happy and utterly at peace. We had everything we ever wanted and so, so much more beyond what we could have ever imagined. We had no spiritual or material longings or unsatisfied desires – a look, a touch, or a kiss from each other is all we ever needed. Irene could just sit beside me and I could feel a deep calm flow across my body and mind bringing me totally to peace and happiness.

As the nature of our lives changed over time, our relationship just grew to find new ways of showing our love for and enjoying each other. The more things changed, the more we learned about each other and saw who each other truly was over time … which made us fall even deeper and more completely in love. Later in our marriage, when my three biological children moved back to the area, they all became close with Irene and that was just one more thing I found to love about her. I considered her children mine, and she considered mine to be her own. We never used the term "step" to introduce or talk about them to others.

As alike as we are in many ways, we also have different but complimentary aspects in other ways. She is outspoken, very friendly and social; I am quiet and keep to myself. People gravitate to Irene; generally, people tend to avoid me. She is very intuitive and has an immense amount of faith; I am more logical and am always trying to figure things out in advance. Over time we have learned quite a bit from each other, but more than anything we learned to completely trust and have faith in each other regardless of where that led.

We can sit for hours just talking, or sit for hours saying nothing. A touch or a glance, for us, can say everything we need to hear. We could just sit and look into each other's eyes. I think we talk mostly because we love each other's voices.

That's what it's like for us. I tell you these things so you might be able to imagine what it would feel like, what it should feel like, when your eternal, beloved soul-mate – your other half – dies. I present this to you so that you might understand the remarkable nature of what we accomplished after she passed from this world and how it is I was not destroyed by overwhelming grief. In addition, it was accomplished without any esoteric spiritual abilities like being able to leave my body and visiting her in Heaven, or hearing her voice, or even having her appear to me in dreams.

It is possible to continue your relationship with your loved ones after they pass from this world - if that is what you want to do. In so doing – I believe, as it happened for me – it is possible to greatly alleviate the grief and pain we endure, and how long it must be endured. It may even be possible to feel happy and whole again. You might even be able to feel joy – not a joy tempered by underlying sadness, but a joy made all the better by an underlying excitement and anticipation for what the two of you still have and will have in the future.

Irene and I were committed to taking care of the other in the event one of us passed away, and we found ourselves in the kind of afterlife we believed existed. Whichever of us passed first would stay and help take care of the other and our children from the other side. We had long known that we were soul-mates and we were together forever. We had planned on treating death as just another challenge we would overcome.

However, formulating and agreeing to such a plan, and thinking a thing possible is much different from carrying out that plan in the face of such a traumatic event. Emotions can simply overwhelm you. The physical world has a way of beating you into conformity because it can be relentless. I had several factors working in my favor that many people may not have, but that doesn't mean the same kind of results aren't possible for you, only that they may be more difficult to achieve.

For many of us who have seen our true soul-mate pass, the only options are to either live for the rest of our days in despair and mind-crushing, heartbreaking pain, or to find some way back to that deep, fulfilling connection. Some may think I am living in a fantasy, but no mere fantasy could put an end to my grief and fill me with joy and the deep sense of her presence. You can't lie your way out of profound grief. For some of us, the only thing that will end the grief is experiencing that connection, that relationship again. Trying to find my way back to a real connection with her was the only pathway available to alleviate the unbearable burden of pain and be truly happy again – even joyful - with every thought I have of Irene.

However, "believing it" is not a necessary preliminary aspect of regaining the joyful and fulfilling nature of your relationship, if that is what you choose do – or must do, to have any semblance of a good life. While I hoped it was possible, I didn't really believe it could happen until I started actually experiencing periods of time, after the grief had kicked in, where I was happy and felt connected to her. When I began experiencing her presence, her signs, and that beautiful connection, doubt was quickly laid to rest, grief dissipated and no scar was left on my heart.

Chapter 2
Special Circumstances

I've described how Irene and I already believed in afterlife interaction and wanted to develop our communication after one of us crossed over to help the other. In addition to that belief and agreement, there were other aspects of our particular situation that have helped me immensely in moving forward through the grief and in getting to a place where the grief is gone, and where sadness related to her passing is rare.

First, I have a living situation that is conducive to my efforts to keep my relationship with Irene strong. I live alone (since Irene passed) and in a small, quiet town. I work from home and set my own hours. This meant that any time I needed to pray, meditate, or have a grief-stricken breakdown, I could; I didn't have to bottle anything up. Also, I could talk out loud without anyone overhearing and interfering, something I personally found to be very useful. Talking to Irene out loud made her presence seem more real to me. Sometimes I would roam the house praying or speaking affirmations out loud. I would repeat reassurances to myself, such as, "Irene is right here; she's doing all she can; we will get through this; have faith," over and over, sometimes quite loudly as if to drown out my pain and grief, or to force such thoughts into my mind and body. Later it was so beneficial to be able to just talk out loud to Irene and others that might be helping me out. Interacting "out loud" was easier and more natural than trying to work through a discussion in my mind. Actually talking helped to gain some distance from some of the grief-stricken chaos going on inside my head. It was a steadying activity.

Second, I have a long history of meditation and "spiritual" thought. I learned meditation when I was a teenager and knew some yoga exercises good for circulation and clearing the mind with breathing. I didn't drink or do any drugs. I was already aware of some dietary considerations that might aid me in my efforts to contact Irene – such as keeping away from refined sugar, which helps in quieting the mind. I also stayed away from red meat and carbs, which can cause me to be drowsy and have difficulty meditating.

Third, I was already familiar with many good resources for afterlife research and other related materials, so I knew where to look for support and information. Fourth, I actually have a supportive family that made it that much easier on me to go down this path. I have family I can depend on if I need them for anything.

Another thing that those of us alive at this time in history have that so many that came before us never had is access to information. With a few keystrokes you can find a lot of information about anything on the internet. You can find and download books to read on your computer or tablet – books that you would never be able to find before in most areas of the world. Not just books, but videos, research, even groups dedicated to afterlife studies. It's really the best time and place to be alive to make this kind of an effort.

Additionally, Irene crossed over after a thirty month fight with cancer, so she and I had all the opportunity we needed to make sure we said everything that needed to be said. We always told each other how much we loved each other. We also talked about our plan - if she passed over, she would be doing everything she could to take care of us and let us know she was okay, and to stay near me to try and keep our relationship strong and positive until I could join her.

As you can see, I had a lot going for me when my wife passed from this world on Tuesday, April 11, 2017. We had long since said everything that needed to be said and everything we wanted each other to know; there were no regrets. It wasn't an unexpected passing and Irene had already said several times that she was growing very tired of the pain and the fight against the cancer. In life, she had everything she ever wanted – all her dreams and desires had come true. We all gave her our blessings, at the end, to go on from this world.

This was about as "good" a situation as one can be in to endure the passing of any loved one, let alone your soul-mate - at least for me personally. Perhaps others wouldn't like being alone in a big house, but for me it was an important part of my personal effort. I'm also in decent health and, for whatever reason, was able to sleep easily almost every night after Irene passed. I don't know if that was comfort extended from the other side or not, but it's almost impossible for me to function positively without a good night's sleep.

I don't think, however, that any of the above special circumstances are absolutely necessary to achieve a positive, fulfilling relationship with a loved one who crossed over, although in my case I felt they were very helpful. I think there's a process one can use to get to that point regardless of virtually any circumstance.

Chapter 3
Grief

I believe I've developed a basic process by which one can accomplish the transition from grief when our loved ones pass from this world to some degree of happiness, functionality, normalcy and even joy. How far one goes depends on the individual and their beliefs, their particular physical circumstances and how willing they are to go where the process leads them. There are a lot of potential problems - physical and psychological - that are working against us in such a situation that are difficult to overcome.

The first obstacle is just the sheer physiological withdrawal one goes through. I don't think it can be avoided other than by some sort of grace or transdimensional power. I was "given" a couple of weeks of grace after Irene died where I felt then pretty much like I do now, or even better. From that, I knew it was at least possible to feel whole, happy and connected to Irene even though she had crossed over.

I call it "withdrawal" because when I started feeling the grief, I started comparing it to going into withdrawal after going cold turkey after twenty-seven years of being addicted to what was, for me, the most wonderful drug in the world - my wife, Irene. When she was in this world, whenever I looked at her, I felt the rush of overwhelming love; whenever I was near her, I felt this soothing sense of peace and contentment. I could think of her and feel joy.

Obviously, Irene is much more than just a physical presence, but that physical presence is something we become dependent upon. Psychologically, we know they are always nearby and that we can see and touch and talk to them any time we want, and that provides a great comfort and happiness. In this world, these relationship sensations and experiences are expressed chemically in our bodies. We develop an intense physico-chemical symbiosis with certain loved ones. If you take that person away physically, then it is going to have a profound effect on us physically and, if we believe we cannot see, touch, or hear them ever again, the psychological effect can be devastating, which compounds the physical withdrawal. Irene is more than just a physical or psychological presence. "The whole is greater than the sum of its parts," as the saying goes, and we are connected to our loved ones in ways we cannot see and do not realize in the normal course of our lives.

Grief is not to be confused with normal sensations of emotional pain, loss, and sorrow. When Irene died, I had already lost my mother, father and brother. Of those three the most loss I felt was when my mother passed, but that was because we were taking care of her in our home towards the end of her life. She was in my life every day, and so I was used to her being there. However, I still didn't feel grief at her passing.

It's not that I didn't love them, but I already had a deep conviction that there was an afterlife and that they were fine and enjoying their afterlife pursuits. My spiritual, emotional, psychological and physical relationship with them was not powerful enough to affect me like Irene's passing affected me because she and I are deeply connected on all levels and have been for a considerable time. I already believed Irene was fine after she died. I fully believed she was on the other side, interacting with us and helping us, but believing that had no power over the sheer physiological withdrawal due to her physical absence.

I compare grief to withdrawal for this reason: it appears there's just no stopping it with psychological or spiritual tools or beliefs, at least for some length of time. You have to go through it (and it may be that some of us come here specifically to experience it.) It is relentless physically, emotionally and psychologically. It is why they lock you up in a facility where you are monitored when you go through chemical withdrawal; you cannot think normally. It's like going mad, and that's on top of the abject sorrow and sense of loss. I would have uncontrollable fits of sobbing and experience pain unlike anything else. Even while I knew she was okay and was still with me, even after she gave me all sorts of amazing signs from the other side, I still experienced shattering grief.

Many people never recover from this; they feel grief over the loss of their loved one, to some degree, the rest of their lives. It can leave a wound that never heals. It can literally kill you by damaging your heart and physical system so much. One of the worst things about grief can be the sense that your loss cannot ever be recovered; that is a horrible, maddening sensation.

The process that I describe in this book doesn't prevent grief when your loved one dies. It cannot, in my opinion, because that physiological withdrawal is going to occur no matter what we do. The process I'm going to describe can, I believe, help get one through that grief, perhaps mitigate it to some degree, shorten its duration and deliver one to normalcy on the other side where the grief has not even left a scar. It may be unbelievable at this point if you are currently experiencing grief, but this process delivered me to a place where my relationship with Irene, my sense of happiness, satisfaction, joy and love were even better than before. In addition, I have developed an excited anticipation about our future together using this process. Day by day, week by week, I felt better and better, well beyond anything I had thought realistically possible, especially not in so short a time.

I put this process together via trial and error while I was going through the grief because I was desperately trying just to survive and figure out some way to continue living, with the hope that I could get back to how I felt those first two weeks. That's what the two weeks of grace in the beginning gave me that perhaps many don't have - the hope that there was some way to get through the grief and recover, somehow, my relationship with Irene and all the existential peace it provided me.

Looking at grief as a form of addiction withdrawal was helpful in the process, because it framed what I was experiencing as something I could eventually get through and get past. All I had to do was survive long enough and that part of what I was experiencing would eventually stop. However, I also knew that unless I found a way to continue my relationship with Irene, I would never recover to the point where I could actually enjoy the rest of my life. While I might have been able to stagger through the rest of it, painfully and sorrowfully, there would always be a deep wound that would not be healed by time. Time does not heal all wounds, although it may make them bearable.

Some deaths you cannot put behind you and "move on" because you know, deep in your heart, there is nothing and no one else that can fill that missing part of you. Nothing can even cover it up or successfully distract you from it. It must be that person. You must have that person in your life. It didn't seem possible to me, especially in the midst of experiencing grief, that there would be any way to heal that wound without being able to physically touch, see, and hear Irene either here or perhaps through astral projection, leaving my physical body temporarily and interacting with her in the astral planes. At the very least I thought I would need some very realistic, interactive dreams of her on a regular basis.

As I found out, though, none of those more esoteric spiritual occurrences were necessary to completely relieve me from my devastating grief and deliver me to a state comparable to my state of mind prior to her passing. Actually, the process put me into an even better state of mind, considering how worried I was during the thirty months she was sick with cancer and how much it pained me to see her go through that. Now, I know she is perfectly healthy, young again, and full of energy; so that makes me very happy for her - and it's a huge relief and source of peace and joy for me.

An important note here: if you do not believe in an afterlife where our loved ones can survive and can, to some degree, contact us and interact with us while we are still here - leaving us signs, coming to us in dreams, talking to us or giving us feelings or intuitions in our minds, I don't know that what this book offers will help you. All of my efforts sprang from my long-held belief that we survive death and live in a relatively Earth-like world afterward, from which we have the capacity to interact here to some degree. I also believed Irene and others were actively helping me from the other side. If you want some some information to help you acquire such a belief, I suggest the following resources:

Soul Smart *by Susanne Wilson*
Understanding Life After Death - *by Cyrus Kirkpatrick*
A Lawyer Presents the Evidence for the Afterlife *by Victor Zammit*
The Realities of Heaven *by Miles Allen*
Afterlife Research by the University of Virginia Medical Center - *Video*
The Scole Experiments - *Video*

Chapter 4
The Process

Know The Goal

Something important I learned along the way was to understand what I really wanted and focus on that, and not on what I thought I had to do before I could get what I wanted. For a long time I thought I must astral project to her world in order to achieve a satisfying relationship, and so I focused on learning to astral project. I was stymied again and again in my efforts to astral project - couldn't breath, my throat would get real dry, my allergies would act up - I literally couldn't lie down to try it without something cropping up.

What I realized was that I was focusing on what I thought was a necessary intermediary step and not the thing I wanted itself. As it turns out, I didn't need to astral project; I didn't need vivid dreams of her; I didn't need to hear her voice or feel her touch to defeat the grief and experience that deep connection to her to return me to a joyful state.

The first step of the process is to know the goal. If you are in the midst of grief, this in itself might be difficult. You might think your goal is to be able to hear their voice and feel their touch; you may think your goal is to have vivid dreams of them, but these are not really your goal. What your goal really is, is to feel good again - to feel whole and complete again, happy and joyful, satisfied that your loved one is still with you and that you have a future with each other to delight in - or something along those lines. The goal is to defeat the grief and the sorrow and have that happy relationship back and be able to go forward with it.

Put aside any ideas or beliefs that it is not possible - it is. Many others and I have done exactly that. Don't try to figure out how it's going to happen; this will only lead to confusion and self-imposed limitations. It reduces what can be done for you (by helpers in the astral) and by you during the process. Just establish your goal without any judgements or further assessment so you can focus on that and not on things that might distract and lead you down blind alleys. Let God, the responsive nature of the universe and those on the other side who are helping you take care of all the particulars - including putting whatever you need to do in front of you in a way that you will recognize it.

Focus On The Goal

This might be especially hard when experiencing grief, but what needs to be done is to find some way to focus on the goal. I used both prayer and affirmations initially, and I used them constantly, to the point of driving all other thoughts out of my mind. I prayed loud and often and walked around repeating affirmations, through tears and between sobs.

An example of my early affirmations, taken from my blog, which I would repeat like a mantra to fight against the pain and chaos in my head:

"I love you so much, Irene, and I know you love me. We are soul mates. We will always be together. We are happy. We are joyful. We feel fulfilled and whole. I experience you, sense you and know you are here with me at all times. You are right here with me. We are completely connected. Our experience of each other gets better and more clear every day. This is a very special time in our relationship. We are strong for each other. We are focused for each other. We live every day in each other's heart and mind."

An example of one of my prayers to God, taken from my blog:

"Dear God, grant us the peace, the strength, the comfort and the grace we need to stay strong and keep our hearts and minds free from

pain, suffering, grief, doubt and fear. I know Irene is here with me. I know she is now completely healthy, happy and free from the pain, suffering and fear she had while her body as failing her. Please give me the grace, knowledge and understanding necessary to see her, hear her, feel her, and know without doubt or fear that she is right here comforting us and looking out for us. Dear God, let us go forward continuing our loving relationship with joy and peace in our hearts knowing that we always be together even through obstacles and challenges, because we are soul-mates and our bond of love is the very thing this universe was created for."

An example of an internal dialogue with myself, when feeling down:

"It's okay, we'll get through it, it'll pass, it gets better every day. I can just suddenly feel better for no reason, or tomorrow I may wake up and feel great. It doesn't matter, it will all be okay. I still know you're here, I still know I'll at least see you and hold you again when I die, if not before."

I would make up prayers, affirmations and internal dialogues as I needed them or thought of them. I would try to make them as positive as possible, but sometimes I just begged for relief from the pain and hurt and confusion - there's nothing wrong with asking for help. In fact, I advise asking God and what I refer to as your "spirit team" for help. Asking for help is a clear intention to get past the grief and get to the goal, which is feeling good and connected in a fulfilling, wonderful relationship with your loved one.

Although it might be hard at first, part of focusing on the goal is imagining the goal in a way that generates happiness, joy and excitement. In other words, some way of picturing yourself with your departed loved one that does not compound your grief or cause more bad feelings than good. Do not think of painful memories if you can avoid it; invent new images of them with you in spirit form, or imagine the two of you in Heaven, perfectly healthy, having fun. Imagine they are watching TV with you or they are with you when you drive somewhere - anything, as long as you feel good about it.

What you are doing by focusing on these representations of your goal is using your imagination, words, actions, and thoughts to tune in to the frequency, or the place, where your goal state is a reality. You want to feel good again, so you say words and think thoughts and create images that set your intention towards achieving your goal. Speak affirmations that reprogram your mind towards that goal simply by repeating statements as if you have already achieved your goal. Offer prayers that ask for help achieving that goal, and visualize imagery that produces feelings similar to what you want in your goal situation.

Do not burden yourself with believing it is up to you to figure out how to get from point A to Z. Do not beat yourself up for miscues or perceived failures or weakness. Do not dwell on negative thoughts or sensations, and do not worry about how impossible or difficult the path forward seems to you. Simply focus on the goal in ways that make you feel as good as possible, using words that describe the experience in which you want to exist.

Write It Down

Every day, write down how you feel. If you have a crash, report it in your writing, even if it is just one line or one word. If it's just a day of getting by but not crashing too bad, write it down. Make sure you write down every single good experience, every good feeling. This is important because grief can make you forget and make you believe you never felt good.

I would have really good days where I felt entirely normal and happy. Grief would then hit and I would totally forget about having felt happy, or cause me to believe I was lying to myself. I would go back and read my journal and be totally amazed at how recently I had felt so much better - sometimes it was the day before, and I had forgotten about it! Give more energy and attention to writing down every mote of positive experience and feeling so it helps tune you in to the goal and so you can go back and re-read the positives over and over. Re-reading the positives will help you get through the negative times.

You want to pay particular attention to writing down when you feel good because giving those things your focus and attention tunes you into a frequency that reprograms your mind in a positive way. Writing down your progress also helps maintain the intention that you are going to make progress; it is the reason you are spending time writing it down in the first place. This can be a powerful part of the process.

Sometimes you may feel, when you are writing, that your loved one is trying to write through you. Let them express what it is you think they are trying to say - write it down. At one point in my process it became clear to me that I kept forgetting when I had actually felt good; in my grief I kept insisting that it was all a lie and was fooling myself. I sat down to write a letter to myself so I could read it in the future and at least intellectually cling to the hope that I really did feel good and that it was possible to feel good again.

When I started writing, though, I felt this very insistent urge to begin the letter as if Irene was writing it to me beginning with what she always called me, "Lover," … not exactly something I'd write to myself! Here is the letter I believe Irene wrote to me, through me, that day:

"Lover,

There is a blissful, happy state that you have felt several times since I left the physical. During these times you feel 100% connected to me, without any doubt, grief, fear or sorrow. During these times you feel so joyful, complete and connected with me it is indescribable and makes our hearts explode with love and completeness and clears away all doubt. It is something that your mind cannot accept when you are feeling bad and it tries to persuade you out of your knowledge and memory of this. You know how these negative feelings and entities try to hurt and confuse us when we are moving forward – don't let them stop you! You're doing great! We are on this train together in "perfect accord". I will never, ever leave you. You know this – you are my soul mate, baby, my always. Our reality is better than the fantasy! I am so proud of you, lover. I know it is hard but this is going to get better and better, easier and easier – I promise! - Irene"

Writing that letter was intensely emotional and I felt such relief afterward, it's impossible to fully describe. It was a very important step in moving forward and was not something I had planned out or even felt like I directed while writing. It just came pouring out of me. If this happens to you, don't worry about whether or not it "sounds" like your loved one, because what they are saying is being interpreted and expressed through your mind; pay attention to what it feels like. While I was writing that, it completely felt like I was tuning in to Irene and writing what she wanted me to express. Whenever I read it, even months later, it has the same emotional impact on me.

Talk To Your Loved One(s), Imagine They Are With You

Every day, as much as possible, try to talk to your departed loved one in as normal a way as possible, out loud and in your mind. Since she passed over, I always pour my wife a cup of morning coffee and fix it the way she likes it (though now she probably has the very best French Vanilla cappuccino every morning and I joke with her about my ritual). Just like I always did, I set it down on the coffee table in front of her spot on the couch, pour my own cup and sit next to her and just start talking to her. I imagine her sitting there with me, talking with me, just as we always did.

We always watched Wheel of Fortune, so I still sit and watch it with the belief that she is next to me, talking about the same things we always used to during the show. A new thing we've started doing together is when I go out and smoke a cigarette on the swing in the front yard a couple of times a day and have long conversations or even just quiet time together. I know she loves being outdoors and she couldn't go outside during the last months, so I try to do more outdoor things with her now that she is free of those limitations.

Using your imagination to picture your loved one and to talk with them tunes you into their afterlife dimensional frequency. What we call "the imagination" is a mental tuning mechanism. It is likely that you are already well tuned in to your loved one, depending on how close you were in life. Using your imagination in the above way is a process of continuing that connection and strengthening it by focusing on it with word, thought, writing and visual imagination.

Find subjects that are happy and fun and light-hearted to talk about. Use your mind to imagine them in a way that doesn't hurt. Tears of joy or happiness or laughter are good, but try not to dwell on that which fills you with sorrow, confusion or leads back to grief. Imagine them talking happily to you, being your guardian angel, your private, unseen beloved - whatever resonates with you and makes you feel the best. Let them tell you their jokes or make their smart-aleck comments that make you smile. If you can do it without too much pain, imagine you and your loved on someplace good, happy and joyful, and tell them how happy you are to see them. Tell them you love them. Tell them you are going to keep talking to them, and you want to keep your relationship going. Tell them you believe the two of you can do it; it's just going to take some time and effort.

It doesn't matter if you say the same things over and over again - there's a reason why spiritual traditions, self-help disciplines and religions are full of repeated mantras, self-dialogue affirmations and prayers: they tune you in to that which you seek and reprogram your mind and body to be in tune with that which you are seeking.

Over time you'll get into the habit of this and things will get better because you will start to feel their presence and the physical withdrawal will start to recede. You may not even consciously understand why you should be feeling better. You might have whole days when you feel great, and feel connected, then you crash again. There may seem to be no reason for it. It might get pretty chaotic - it did for me.

This is another reason why you need to write these things down; the mind attempts to trivialize and take for granted certain things after a while. After a month of not feeling grief and being mostly happy, it occurred to me that I had actually already achieved what I had originally thought probably would never occur. I had already turned my attention to accomplishing a new goal. I went back and checked through my blog to check when I had last recorded a grief episode because it seemed so incredible to me that I could have gone that long without feeling grief.

Conceptualize a Happy, Comfortable Afterlife

Your efforts to "tune in" to the experience of your goal is helped greatly if you act as if (and believe, if you can) that it is real. Having a vague understanding or concept of what your loved one is, where they are and what they are doing doesn't help; it only makes it feel less real. So I'm going to provide here a quick grounding of what I found to be a helpful perspective of what the afterlife is like taken from several books by accomplished mediums, near-death experience and mediumship researcher as well as accounts by credible out-of-body experiencers. You can refer to the resources given at the end of Chapter 3 to read this information for yourself - which I advise. Reading about the afterlife helps you to tune into the frequency you are hoping to acquire - that of having an ongoing, happy, fulfilling relationship with a loved one who has crossed over to the afterlife.

By most accounts, what we call "the afterlife" is simply another dimension of physical-like existence, although it is slightly different at the subatomic/quantum scale. This relatively minor difference at that scale makes for some interesting and significant differences in how those who cross over experience that physical dimension compared to experiencing this one.

First, the afterlife dimension most commonly experienced upon crossing over just feels better. It has a more comforting and loving normal sensation to it. It is a quite a bit more responsive to consciousness, thought and intention, but it feels every bit as solid as this one, and feels even more real. Visitors there often refer to it as a "hyper-real" state, and upon returning feel like this world is less real in comparison. It is not dream-like or what we usually imagine when we think of a "spirit realm".

Making the transition is like taking off a diving suit. Your more refined body, which is what is used in the afterlife realms, is more responsive to thought and appears as (or soon becomes) an idealized version of your Earthly physical self - meaning, young and perfectly fit. Sometimes the transition requires some convalescence or rest once on the other side to get past what can be lingering impressions and problems carried over from this world. Many credible sources describe healing centers where people that suffered from long-term debilitating disease or died in a sudden and traumatic fashion spend a short time recovering from their Earthly experience.

Something to remember is that we do not become magic, all knowing, or all powerful when we cross over; we are still much the same person. There may be things we remember once we cross over because many if not most of us already had lives there before we ever came to Earth.

What would be the most important thing to you if you were to die and find yourself in such an afterlife? Probably for most, we would be concerned about those we left behind. We have relationships still on Earth, people we love and care about, that we want to make sure are okay.

However, interacting with people still on Earth is an effort and requires both knowledge and skill. Your departed loved one might be able to contact you in various ways immediately; they may not. Please be patient with them. However, because the mind is more powerful and influential there, and because they share a deep love connection with you, they can always hear you when you direct your attention towards them and speak either in your mind or out loud.

While our "departed" loved ones can also mentally talk to us at any time, the problem is that we have a hard time understanding and validating them. We don't know how to discern between what they are telling us in our mind and what we are inventing out of our own needs and desires. Some of those references I provided at the end of Chapter 3 will help with that.

The afterlife world most who leave here encounter is much like Earth - cities, homes, nature, even business and industry, although such are not run on economic models but rather by those wanting to make things for others. Although you don't need to, you can eat and drink if you want - we have all the same working parts there as we do here, if not exactly used the same way or for the same reasons. For instance, food and drink are experienced more like consumption art, an experience of taste, flavor and texture much like paintings and music are used to delight our sense of sight and hearing. It's all very familiar and very real, though, and seems natural to us once we are there.

On the other side, a large number of people are very interested in being able to contact people here on Earth and they will be available to help your departed learn how if they do not already know how. Now, there is far, far more in the extra-dimensional planes of existence than the one I'm describing; but for most people here, we go to this nearby and familiar place simply because it is where most of us by far came from and the one most of us resonate with because it is so familiar and like our existence here.

The point here is to give you a rough outline of how to visualize the afterlife dimension your loved one is in so that you can picture yourselves together there in beautiful, enjoyable environments and situations. I love imagining Irene and myself on the beach, or enjoying a swim in a pool, or visiting big, beautiful carnivals with fantastic rides, going to dances, playing the games we used to play, etc. It is comforting and joyful for me to imagine us together in this way, and it is easy to use what is a familiar kind of setting to produce the directional emotions that help take me to my goal.

The best part about this is that this scenario is backed up by the most credible afterlife research and information available, so you can rest assured you're not imagining the impossible or even the unlikely; you're actually imagining what is very likely to be part of your life in the astral/heavenly world.

There are actually endless dimensions and universes in what we call "the afterlife". The Earth we consider the normal world is just one of countless dimensions and realities that exist, so calling "everything but Earth" the "afterlife" is a rather huge misconception. Earth is a place we come for various reasons, but it's hardly a dimension that deserves the term "the normal world," being a very small part of all that exists.

If the particular dimension of the "afterlife" I have painted for you to imagine as part of the process doesn't appeal to you, then imagine whatever gives you comfort because that also surely exists in the infinite expanse beyond this particular world. What is important is that you tune in to whatever frequency helps you to connect to your loved one, including whatever context you imagine to be happiest for the two of you to be in.

Empower Your Loved One(s)

Thoughts and emotions are energies which affect everything around us and especially that which we are connected to through bonds of experience and attachment. Some thoughts and emotions are disruptive and disabling; others are empowering and supportive. This is why it is so important to try to focus on things that make you feel happy and joyful, and if that's too difficult, simply keep repeating affirmations and prayers for and about happiness and joyfulness even through tears and emotional pain.

Laughter and light-heartedness, love and a kind heart are very, very powerful energies. Try to think of things that include your loved one that make you smile and laugh. Or, simply engage in activities that promote a sense of fun and laughter and do so knowing such energies will help your loved one and make it easier for them to interact with you.

Sometimes during grief it may feel disrespectful or hurtful to feel joy and happiness, to have fun and laugh, as if you are not honoring your love and their importance to you. There are a lot of confusing and conflicting emotions one experiences going through grief that are often overwhelming; sometimes it's all you can do just to claw yourself through another day without doing anything self-destructive or inadvisable. The best I could manage on some days was just to repeat prayers and affirmations while going through the worst of it, staying in bed most of the time.

However, there are also times I could laugh with her, play with her, poke fun at my doubts and insecurities, even engage in sarcastic exchanges in my head. I would imagine her saying something like "Are we having a pity party today?" It would always make me laugh, even through tears. One of our favorite things to say was the ever-popular "Get up and rub some dirt on it; you're fine!" Another thought that I began using after I saw a documentary about the lives of some Burmese children who dug snakes out of holes all day long so their family could eat was, "Could be worse, Babe, I could be digging snakes out of holes all day long. In the rain. While hungry."

There are many things to think positively about - such as modern comforts and our ability to find groups and people and materials that can support virtually anything we need or in which we take an interest. There is a proliferation of afterlife materials from very credible researchers to help us feel comfortable and intellectually satisfied that maintaining our relationship with our loved ones who have crossed over is not only possible, but actually probably a more natural and healthy way to go about dealing with the death of people close to us. Our loved ones absolutely enjoy our continued, positive, loving and fun thoughts and interaction as our relationships move forward with them.

Since our relationships with our loved ones do not end when they die, the only question is: what kind of relationship will we have with them? Will it be a painful one full of a sense of loss or a happy, joyful one full of the sense of continued adventure towards a wonderful future? Focus on the latter. Do things that help you focus on the positive so that you can become a source of good energy for your loved one. Such good feelings and emotions change your frequency state to one that resonates more closely to them and allows them easier access.

Think of it this way; a mindset of painfully being without them makes you resonate at that frequency. Resonating at such a frequency makes it hard for your loved ones to get through to you because it's like trying to communicate through two entirely different channels. They are trying to bring comfort and love, joy and happiness, but cannot do that through a pain- and sorrow-laden frequency. Our job is to try and tune ourselves into a frequency that welcomes the sense of peace and continued, positive relationship they want to bring to us.

Acknowledging signs and confirmations when you receive them is another part of encouraging and empowering your "departed" loved ones. Make sure that you let them know when you see a sign or get a confirmation from them about something you have asked them. If something feels to you like is a sign of their presence to you, it likely is and thank them for it. Accept, appreciate and acknowledge all information, help, signs, confirmations, dreams and other interaction. It not only makes them happy, it increase our connectivity. Don't worry about being "wrong" or mistaking a coincidence for a sign, it doesn't matter if you get a few wrong. It's the sense of appreciation, wonder, happiness and connection that these events aid that is important. It will help build the connection.

Trust the Process

One of the things I've discovered through this process and have written about on my blog is that we can change the frequency at which we are resonating. The problem is largely one of conceptualization and this perspective usually lies in a deeply-rooted worldview. Many of us don't even recognize that we have a worldview - we're too busy just living our life to recognize that we live our life in accordance with certain deep beliefs about what life is, what we are, and how things work. Many of us just assume those beliefs represent reality without ever even thinking much about those beliefs.

However, we can change how we think about ourselves, everything around us and reality itself. What I do is think about everything in terms of frequencies I can either tune in or tune out via deliberate mindfulness. Have you ever had something happen to you and all of a sudden it's like you've become someone else? You can't stop thinking about it and it adversely affects you physically? Or, for some reason, everything seems to be going against you, or going your way? When things happen to us, most will react to that occurrence by habit; seeing it a certain way, interpreting it a certain way, responding our usual way, never giving it a second thought because we think all of that simply represents reality. What other way would you respond? What other way is there to look at it? You may be so committed to your frequency as reality that even the thought that there are other ways to see or interpret a thing is unthinkable, and that anyone who doesn't see it your way is either a fool or crazy.

It can be hard to dig ourselves out of a frequency we are committed to because how we resonate in that frequency has become who we are, and we cannot conceive of ourselves being any other way. It may be a deep part of our resonating frequency that there really is no afterlife, or that there really is no way to actually communicate with our loved ones that have died, and that sense of loss and separation will be a part of our lives until we die because there is no way to remove those sensations from that frequency.

To maintain or develop a satisfying, joyful relationship with our loved ones on the other side, it may be necessary to change some fairly fundamental parts of yourself. This may not be easy, and it could cause some rough sledding. The good news, however, is that you don't have to figure out what you need to change. You don't have to weed out psychological issues and resolve them. That would be a virtually endless and tiresome task.

No, all you need to do is focus on the frequency you want (that emotional feeling) and keep doing the process as I've described. Whether you believe in it or not is irrelevant because what you are doing in the process is re-writing your "programming" at a fundamental level, and this will also change the beliefs that are necessary to accomplish the new goal.

We cannot just tell ourselves to believe or not believe a thing out of the blue. Finding a thing "believable" depends on how well it comports with our internal programming and narrative. People can deny the obvious or accept the most bizarre things as true, and they can do so because of their "programming" - the internal dialogue and narrative that sorts, categorizes, justifies, and interprets everything we experience.

The technique here is to bypass the belief (and disbelief) barrier via affirmation, repetition, imagination, emotional connection, intention, etc., which over time naturally changes the programming and internal dialogue and mental processing. That in turn changes what we find believable and changes the narrative we hold on a very deep level that guides our thoughts. We are bypassing our existing programming and reprogramming ourselves according to our own desires and goals. This way, you don't ever have to concern yourself with the idea that perhaps you don't "believe" in the idea of afterlife communication enough to have success.

I never believed, for example, that we would be successful in a lot of things things Irene and I accomplished both while she was alive and afterward, but what I didn't do was stop using affirmation, visualization and doing whatever was in front of me to do. I didn't let myself get in the way by giving up on the process. I never expected to be able to defeat my grief, although I hoped; I certainly did not think that a few short months after she passed over I would be happy and joyful with her in our new transdimensional relationship, my grief a thing of the past!

Being receptive to the internal changes in perspective that may happen allows your frequency to change, moving you closer to your goal experience. Accepting internal change empowers the forces and people working to help you towards your desired outcome. Resistance will make that achievement more difficult. Keep in mind that some basic things about you may have to go through change in order to achieve your goal.

Many deep issues in my psychology had to be overcome or laid to rest in order for me to feel whole and happy again, but to get here I didn't dig up fears, pains and insecurities, understand them or have a professional help me lay them to rest. By following the process and focusing on the frequency in which I wanted to exist, all of the psychology took care of itself. I could just feel better without knowing anything about why I felt better or how.

That's not to say that sometimes an intellectual understanding of my issues didn't come to mind. For instance, at one point I realized that I was holding on to pain because it was a powerful connection to Irene and letting go of the pain felt like I was diminishing her importance in my life. Of course, being human, now and then I did try to work things out intellectually, telling myself that she would always be the most important thing in my life, but what had the most effect on letting go of the pain was a thought that just burst into my mind at one point: *"You don't have to be in pain to show me that you still love me."*

It immediately felt to me that Irene had put that thought in my head, and it had a dramatic and immediate effect on me. I kept returning to those words over and over over the course of weeks as I gradually let go of what pain I was subconsciously holding on to. That pain had given me a sense of feeling close to her, of demonstrating my love for her, and I didn't realize it. As I continued the process, I found the ability to feel close to her, to love her without the sense that I should feel pain.

I was able to let go of issues like that not because I was intellectually or psychologically able to "work through the issues," but rather because my focus on the goal moved me through frequencies of mental activity and information where those thoughts and transformations existed along the way, into areas where Irene and others on her side could better communicate with me and give me more help. I received signs and confirmations on an almost daily basis for months as I went through this. It is my opinion that I got so much help from the other side, and experienced so much interaction, because acknowledging them and openly interacting with them was a priority, and it drew me into frequencies where they could do all sorts of things for me.

Trusting this process doesn't mean "do not go to traditional grief counseling"; you can easily do both. However, this book is intended for those who have no intention of "moving on" from loved ones that have crossed over and who choose to try to maintain the relationship going forward. If your grief counselor advocates for something other than this, the two may be working towards incompatible outcomes and you may need to look for other forms of counseling that embrace these kinds of relationships - and yes, there are some such counselors.

Also, every particular about my process may not resonate with you; in my opinion, never agree to something that does not resonate. I am certainly no expert in this - I only have my own experience to offer. To some degree you will have to find your own distinct process that works for you. It may or may not line up entirely with my own.

The main reason I say "trust the process" is that there will be days or even weeks where nothing good seems to be happening and where the grief is unrelenting and almost unbearable. The process is not magic; in my view, it can only move you towards the desired outcome at a certain speed as it guides you through frequencies that make it possible for you to get where you want to go. There's no telling how long that journey will take or exactly how it will progress, but it is my opinion that the process offers the most efficient path towards the goal. It focuses entirely on the goal and not on what may be blind alleys and misdirections if one focuses on the what they think are necessary steps and pathways in-between.

It is my view that God, Source, the universe, your higher self and your afterlife helpers are much better equipped to find the best, most efficient path through the chaotic and confusing maze that grief and such strong emotions present. Having faith and trusting in those influences and powers, and doing your job of simply focusing on the frequency of the goal, offers the best chance of navigating such terrible and dark waters - again, in my opinion. It is for you to make up your own mind and do what you think is best for you.

Chapter 5
Final Thoughts

You can read many more details about my experience at my blog, "Love After Life", at transdimensionallove.com. This is a day by day account of what I went through as (I believe) my spirit team and I worked to get me through my grief and get my relationship with Irene back on a positive, happy and satisfying footing going forward. Again, I don't claim my way will work for everyone, or even for most people. I only offer it as a possible way forward for some who think it might work for them.

When Irene passed over, I didn't feel grief for about two weeks. Instead, I felt like our relationship had simply changed to a new format, and I still felt mostly whole and happy. I felt her presence and talked to her constantly. After that initial two weeks, I plunged into a very dark and despairing grief, which was when I started looking for a way to get back to what I was feeling those first two weeks. Had I not had that initial experience, I don't know what I would have done; because even after having that experience, it was very difficult to have any hope at all during bouts of grief.

Over time, using the process, the grief ebbed and flowed, gradually decreasing in both potency and frequency while the good feelings and experience began to increase. The good experiences brought with them their own emotional and psychological challenges as I had to find a way of being okay with feeling less pain and not feel like I was diminishing my connection to Irene or how important she is to me. Many other issues cropped up, such as how it would hurt when other people would not talk about her or whenever I had to get rid of some of her things. Doing that still hurts, but I found ways and information about the afterlife that helped me to deal with it, which is detailed in the daily account of the blog.

I don't want to get into describing what exactly happened to me and how I dealt with those issues in this book because resolving whatever obstacles you might encounter may not include the same particulars as my own. Tuning into your own "recovery frequencies" will provide you with whatever you need to get through it, tailor made to you and your particular situation.

As my "recovery" progressed, I realized that even though I still had bouts of missing Irene and self-pity, the actual grief was gone. What I was experiencing was just normal emotions and not hopeless, dark despair and agony. My emotions largely leveled out to where they were before Irene died, and my relationship with her felt much more like the relationship we had before, except now it is even more intimate, since we are in each other's minds and hearts in a much more present way and conscious way. Something about this kind of relationship makes it more intensely appreciated and focused on, and so has a new and unique quality to it - almost like a new, tender long-distance but super-intimate relationship full of magic and wonder. It's really very special and unique.

Some may think that I am somewhat delusional or that I'm imagining all this to escape my grief; that is certainly a possibility. Others may insist that this is not a healthy way to go about overcoming grief; to that I say that experiencing mind, spirit, heart and health-destroying grief on a daily basis is far less healthy than believing in the afterlife continuation of our loved ones and our relationship with them. So if I am "fooling myself", so what? It's far, far better than the alternative.

However, I do believe in the afterlife I have depicted and I believe Irene is right here, right now, with me, albeit in a slightly different dimensional state. In my blog I describe actual events that occurred during this process that are very difficult to explain away as imagination or wishful thinking. I'm not claiming these events prove anything, but they do lend fairly good support to the idea that Irene and others helped me through this from the other side. I also link to materials from very credible experiencers and resources that support that premise - and there is a lot of such supporting testimony and evidence - from near-death experiences to out-of-body experiences to research on mediumship.

Again, I don't offer such resources in an attempt to prove that my worldview on the afterlife is factual; I offer such resources so that those who wish to use this process have support for what they are choosing to try and accomplish. Such external verification can help to satisfy us intellectually so our mind doesn't constantly undermine our attempts with doubt. Reading and viewing these resources help to tune us in to the frequency of what we are hoping to bring into reality: a continuation of our life that includes a happy, fulfilling relationship with a loved one that has crossed over.

Good luck in your efforts! We pray for your comfort and peace of mind.

Afterward
Two Years Later

In the two years that have followed the writing and publication of the first edition of this book, quite a bit has transpired. My relationship with my wife has only become better, deeper and more intimate. I've had many experiences with her, including a full astral visitation with her that lasted for about fifteen minutes. Two of my daughters have had full astral visitations with Irene as well, and she appeared the same physically to all of us - same age, same hair length, etc.

The Facebook group Mary Beth Spann Mank and I started, Love After Life, has rocketed to close to five hundred members; that's nearly five hundred people of all ages, backgrounds, professions, ethnicities, genders, sexual orientation and from around the world that have chosen to continue their relationship with their partners who have crossed over.

When we started the group, I was leery about administering over any group on the internet because my long experience in online groups and forums has always been incredibly negative. The reason I agreed to start the group was because I honestly felt that there would be a top membership of maybe a dozen or less people, and that such a small group would be relatively easy to moderate and manage.

I had no idea so many people were searching for support in pursuing and maintaining their romantic relationships with crossed-over partners. Like us, they were looking for relief, safe haven and others who rejected the idea that we must move on or simply live with our grief for the rest of our lives. They wanted respite from the constant pressure to conform, to stop talking about their partners, to re-partner, to "let go."

Even in so-called "spiritual communities," we all faced this same pressure, as if we were violating some kind of universal law, as if our love for, adoration of and commitment to our partners could be a bad thing. Many of us were attacked and vilified in such communities as well as in regular grief communities, not to mention the constant onslaught to conform and "move on" most face from family and friends. The idea that we could overcome the grief and find happiness and satisfaction with our romantic partner, now in spirit, was considered unhealthy, even "impossible." It was as if others found the very idea of continuing our loving relationship beyond the death of our partners, in a joyful and fulling way, somehow offensive.

A weekly part of our group is coming together in an online video teleconference through the Zoom interface. I can't tell you how satisfying it is to watch the progress of members of the group. Mostly, when they first arrive, they can barely speak without breaking down in tears and using their breaking voice to tell us their story. Over time, these deeply grieving individuals often transform right before our eyes, becoming more positive, more hopeful, more open to the possibility that they can reclaim that sense of fulfilled togetherness with their partners. Some have moved out of grief and are experiencing their partners more and more, in many amazing ways. Some have had full astral visitations with their partners; others have seen them here, heard them, felt them. Most of us have dreams of our partners and experience incredible, ongoing signs and synchronicities, many involving other members of the group, demonstrating that our partners are also working together, on their side, for the benefit of members. We have had several third-partner validations of this from various mediums and other sources.

We have mediums in the group, psychologists, former skeptics (about the afterlife) and scientists, people from every walk of life. When you can interact with other people of like mind, who are all very sincere and matter-of-fact, the effect can be transformational.

For whatever historical and cultural reasons, until now the option of simply continuing our relationship with our crossed-over partner has been discouraged, even vilified, or perhaps just never imagined to be an option. It seems obvious to us now, with so much evidence of our continuation after death, of the reality of the afterlife worlds, of the physical reality of their continuation as physical beings in a wonderful post-death experience, with their messages to us, with the testimony of millions of out-of-body and near-death experiences and the confluence of spiritual and scientific ideas and evidence, that this is an available choice. It is an option for those who have no intention or desire to "move on," because they have found that one true love they know is their eternal, twin-flame soulmate. Why would anyone in heaven or on Earth try to discourage such a beautiful thing?

Our main goal is to offer hope and help for those who are enduring the terrible loss of their soul mate or other loved one. We pray for your relief, comfort, and return to a joyful, fulfilling life. - Bill & Irene Murray

Made in United States
Orlando, FL
27 February 2024

44129575R00026